The Woody Allen of cyberspace.

—Maya Lin
architect / artist

Part of the pleasure of reading this book is watching Josh Koppel invent this way of telling a story, and part of the pleasure is wondering how far he can go with it.

—Ira Glass
host of public radio's
This American Life

Intimate and moving throughout, Josh Koppel's GOOD / GRIEF is a light-hearted recasting of Proust for the age of attention deficit disorder.

—Steven Johnson
editor of FEED Magazine /
author of *Interface Culture*

Perennial / Melcher Media

Good / Grief

Josh Koppel

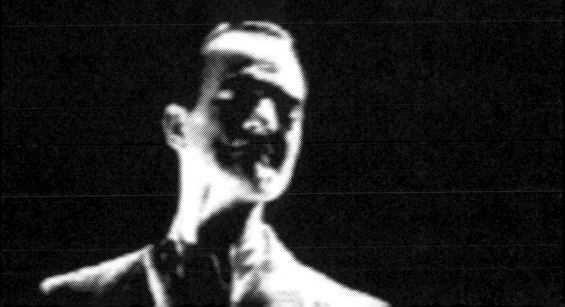
This is me.

I didn't always look this way.

I used to be untouchable.

I was like every other rich kid.

I believed in privilege.   I felt I had earned it.

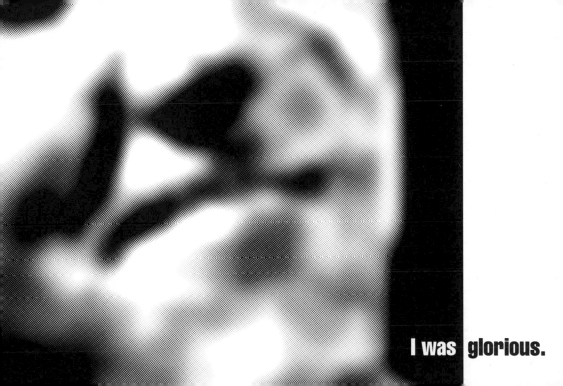

I was glorious.

There were only a handful of people who intimidated me.

One was Daniel Klein,
my childhood nemesis.

I grew up with Dan.

He was one of the beautiful people.

Dan could do anything.

He was really something to see.

He was amazing with women.

And he let you know it.

I used to fantasize about his death.

It made me strong

when I felt puny.

A few years later my family moved away

and Dan became
just another face
that I'd see once
a year

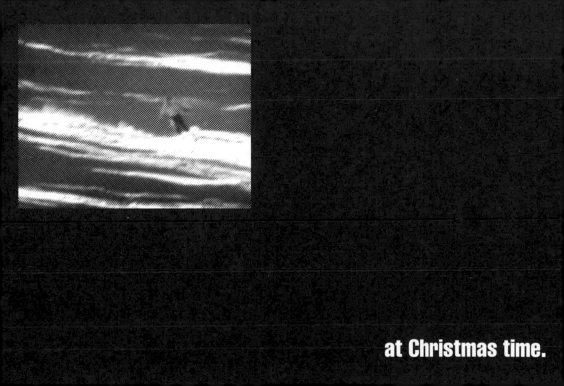

at Christmas time.

When I was seventeen all of our money suddenly ran out.

These words still have
the hint of shame.

My parents could not afford it, but they offered to send me and my brother skiing for Christmas.

But only I took them up on their offer.

I bumped into
Dan and his
brother Aaron
on the mountain
two days before
Christmas.

I always liked being around Dan.

He was really cocky.

We rode up all the chairlifts together

and talked
about manly
things.

It was a perfect day.

And then some time after lunch

I followed Dan down
the mountain.

And he hit a tree.

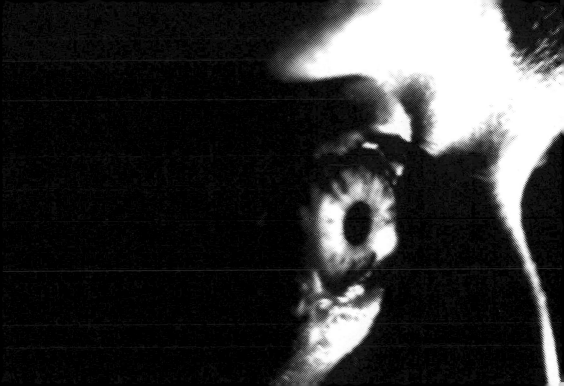

The snow exploded and slowly drifted down over where he lay.

My first
impulse was
to laugh.

He did not get up.

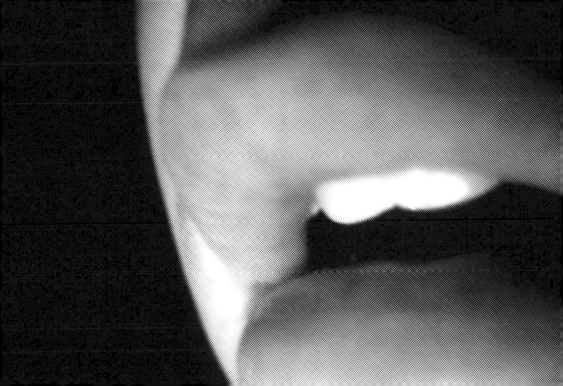

His gloves had been knocked off his hands

and lay in the fresh powder.

We waited in the snow
while the ski patrol
labored to revive him.

I kept waiting for
the happy ending.

His brother
watched
quietly from the
snow bank.

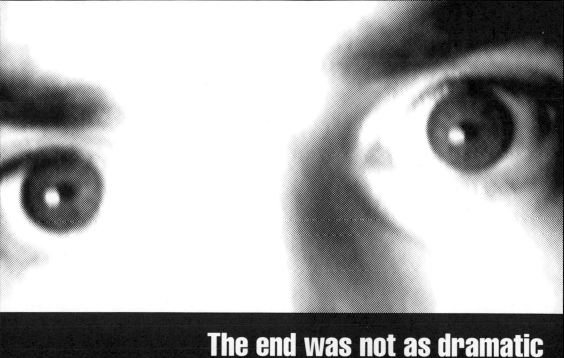

The end was not as dramatic

as I had imagined as a child.

It was quiet.

I chose not to follow them to the hospital.

I went back to the lodge.

Later that day, I spoke to a nurse who told me,

"Mr. Klein wanted you to know that Dan did not live."

When I heard this, all I could do was watch TV.

I called my parents and
my mother screamed so
loudly into the phone that
I hung up on her.

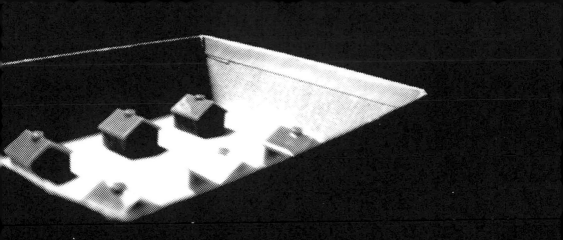

The next day I came home to find his entire town in mourning.

Everyone said that it was a beautiful funeral.

There were so many girls weeping.

I mostly remember
that I kept making
jokes in the car on the
way to the cemetery.

Until my father told me to stop.

"Remember what you see today,"

he whispered in my ear.

I must have told the
story thirty times that day.

I saw his parents at the shiva.

I tried to explain what had happened.

I'm still not so sure myself.

His father hugged
me tightly and
cried into my ear.

He kept touching my face.

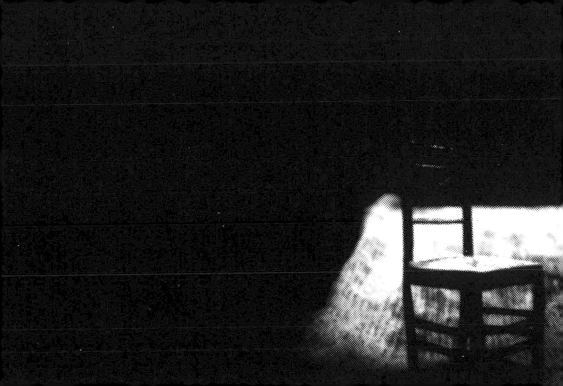

I bump into his family from time to time.

I'm always happy to see them,

but we never talk
for very long.

I never really told them anything.

I found some old dirty magazines in my building storage room this summer.

They had been neatly stashed away on the top shelf by a previous tenant.

I could tell

they had been
there for a long time.

My mother was with
me when I found them.

We laughed about it.

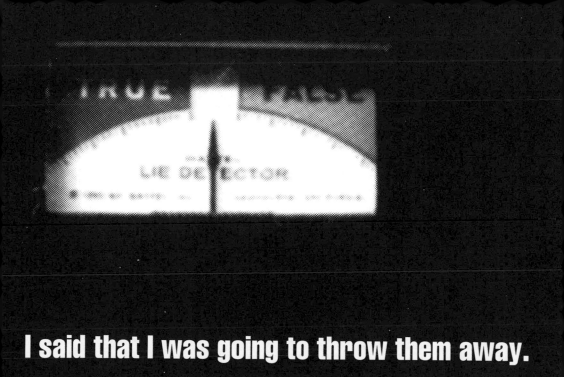

I said that I was going to throw them away.

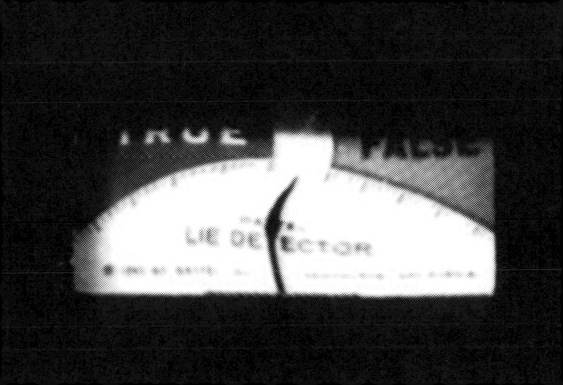

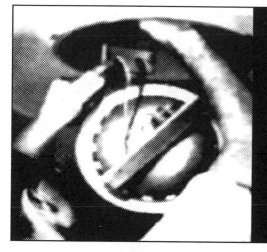

Late at night when the entire house was asleep, I would take them out of my hiding place.

I've always had one of these.

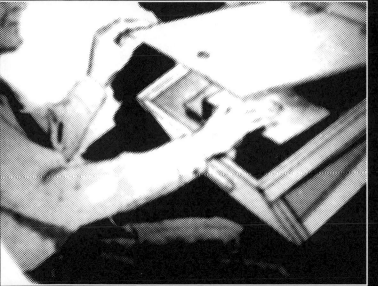

An innocuous looking shelf or drawer,

high above everything else.

I remember finding my father's secret stash one afternoon when I was home sick from school.

It was on a Thursday

when I discovered the new world.

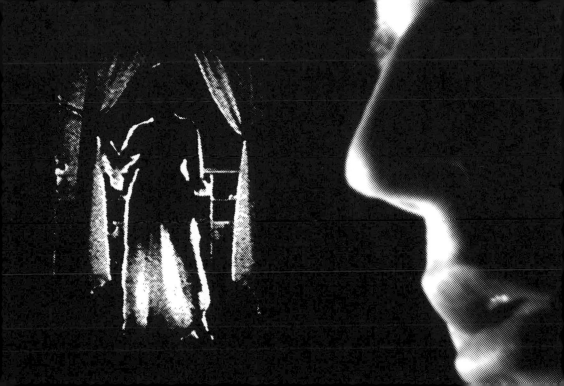

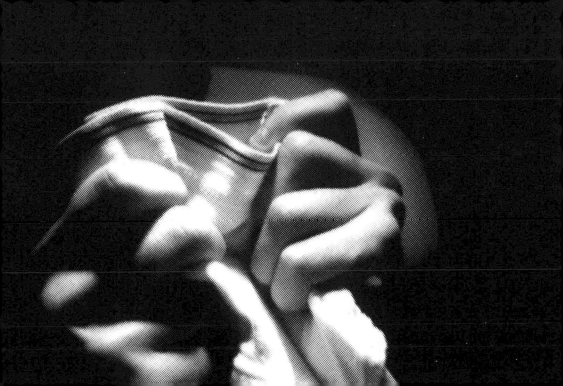

I looked carefully through each page making sure not to miss anything.

MAKE ANYONE
DO ANYTHING
YOU MENTALLY COMMAND
WITH YOUR MIND ALONE

Each page held wonder,

nudity.

My father never
said anything.

Maybe they were there for me to find.

I wasn't about to give them back.

Every day after school I would go into my bathroom and shut the door.

I would look forward to it all day.

We rarely think about being romantic to ourselves.

But I did.

I would bring in food
and other supplies.

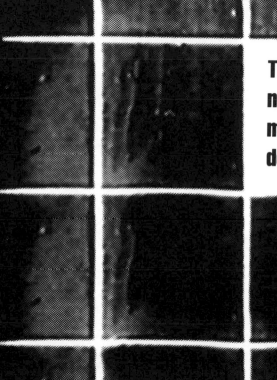

There was no lock on my bathroom door.

So, I devised an elaborate array of early warning detection systems.

They did not always work.

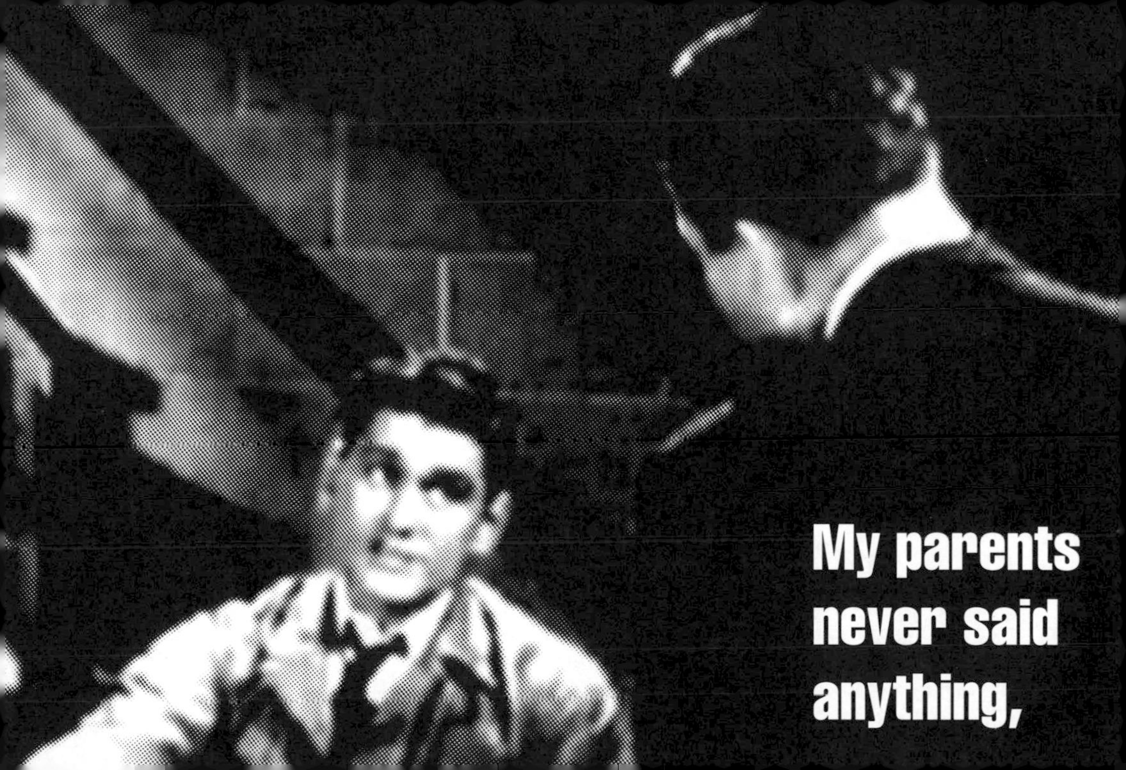

My parents never said anything,

but I spent the majority of my early teenage years in the bathroom.

Around this age, kids often get ultra hygienic.

knew the magazines cover to cover.

I practically memorized all of the dirty letters.

"When I asked my boyfrie[nd] where it was, he gave me a[...] strange look, then he to[ld] me where he left it: up my ass!"

I had my own harem.

Lana

Keisha

I cherish them all.

This first glimpse

of adulthood.

My favorite parts of the
magazines have always
been the ads in the back.

When the pictures
get too graphic,
they put a little
black dot in front
of the action.

WHITE MAN/BLACK WOMAN

Impossible to beat this pure visibility. With the walls

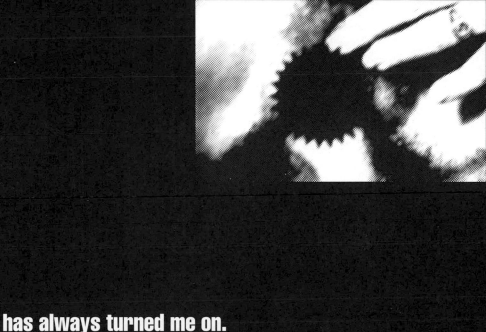

has always turned me on.

As if there are
some acts so
obscene

MEN WHO LOVE WOMEN REL
Watch the young stud
through ALL the
screw up
normal

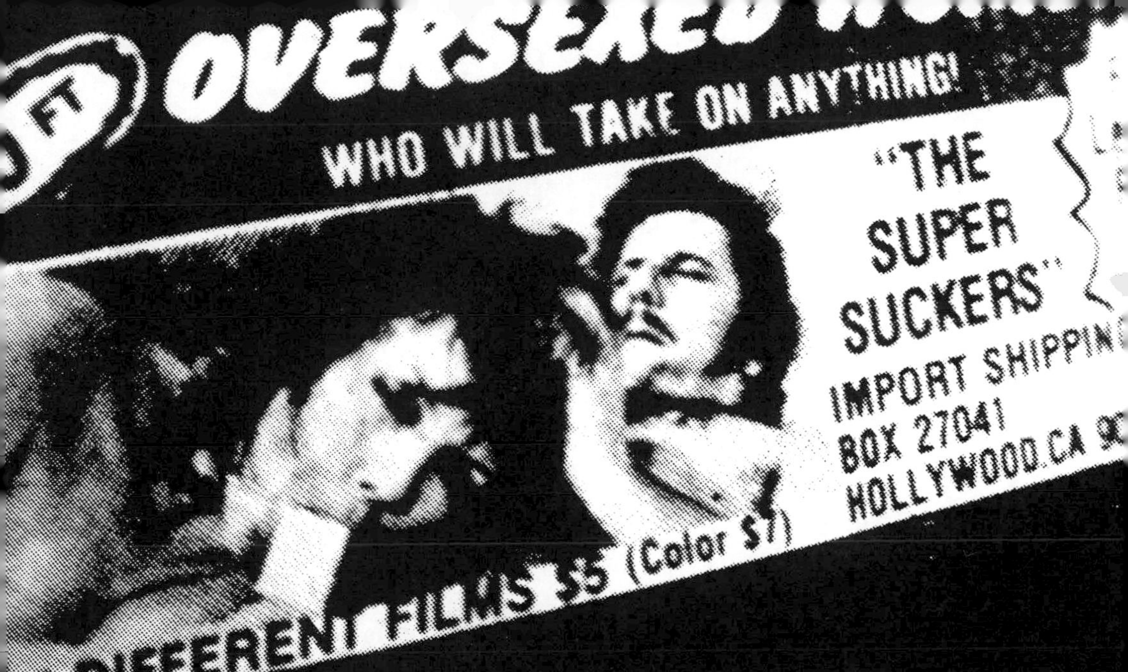

that not even grown-ups are allowed to see.

When I was finally
brave enough to
buy magazines for
myself,

GIANT PHOTO SET $

20 Glossy Photos 1
Full Length Movie

Why? Because we kno
you receive our giant
you'll become a steady c
Let us prove it. RUSH

& ADDRESS TO:

Free

SHOW TIME 6311 Yuc
Hollywod

I got ones with lots of black dots.

I keep them
in a secret place
in my closet,

concealed by the shirts that I never wear.

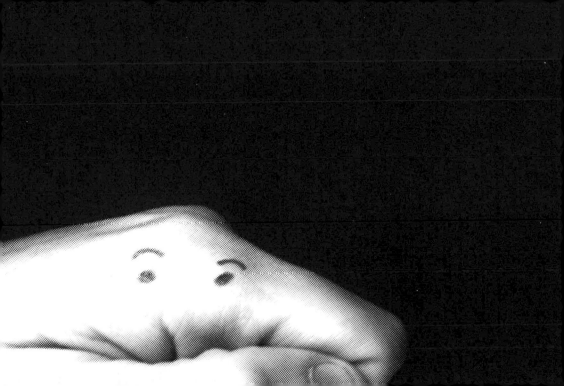

Baby brother.

You are my heart.

The funnest gift

we ever got.

Fully poseable.

And requires no batteries!

Your parents put it together.

Boy

it always made me feel special

that you ran to my bed

for cover

when the monsters came.

And I think you know

your presence in my bed

often sheltered me from my own monsters.

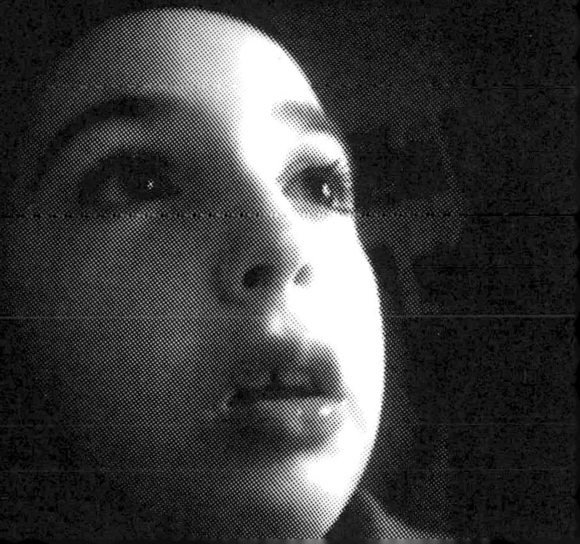

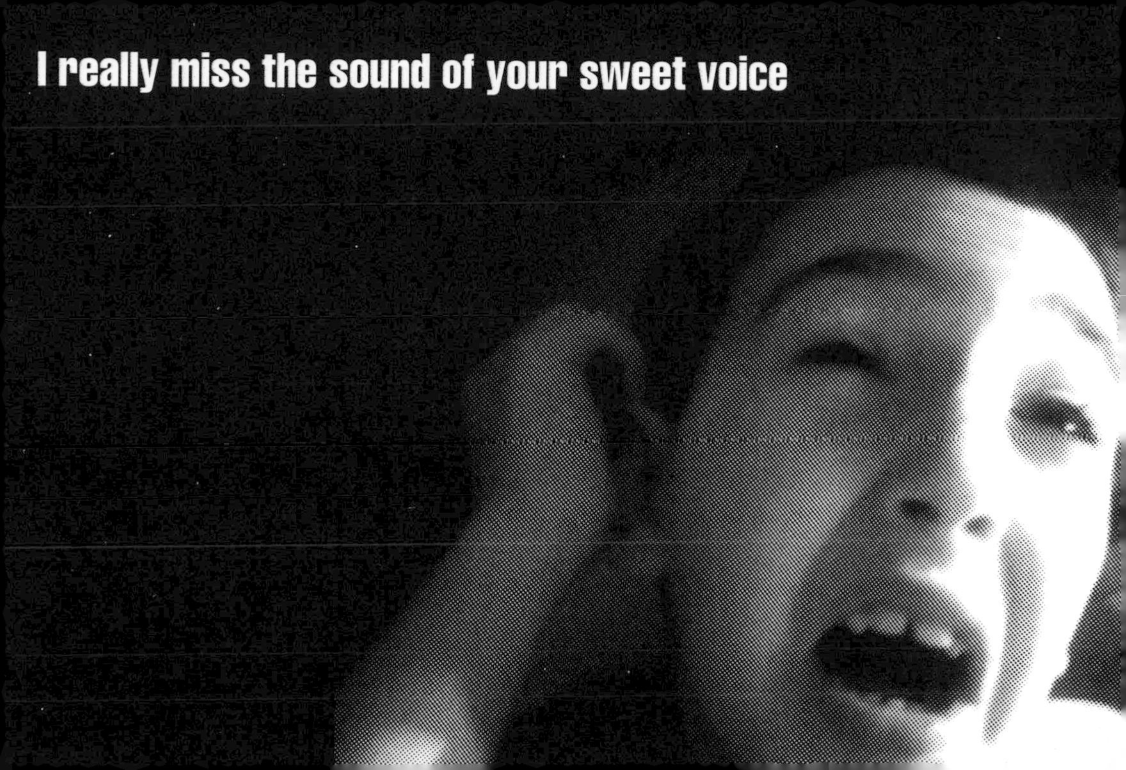
I really miss the sound of your sweet voice

singing movie soundtracks

throughout our happy house.

I've recently learned that

long distance is the bittersweet reality of time.

And even though
I won't always be there
to watch you grow,

I encourage you to memorize my phone number.

Because being your big brother

(and Jonah's too)

is one of my favorite
things in the world.

Love,

Josh

I was driving around.

Had my music playing.

And I looked over at the car next to mine

and saw another student, same as me,

driving through the traffic.

And it hit me.

I'm starting to feel like a grown-up.

way.

So very liberating.

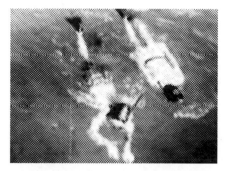

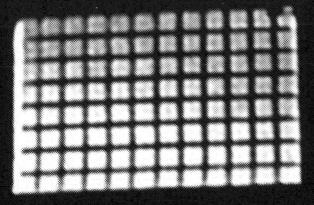

I remember lying in my bed, the day after my 11th birthday party.

and all the boxes
thrown away,

I felt like there was nothing more to look forward to.

It was not a conscious decision,

but I stopped
having birthday
parties after that.

puberty is a word that has always made me uncomfortable.

I was at camp when my body began to change.

**Bodies are
public property
at camp.**

I was the only person up
one Sunday morning,

when I realized
I was sprouting
pubic hairs.

I had been
expecting them
for a while.

But I was really embarrassed.

My body felt totally out of control.

Alien.

I wouldn't talk to anyone about these changes.

I was far too uncomfortable.

I tried to ignore them.

I stopped showering

and I stopped changing my clothes.

But every time I
undressed my body
would be different.

There would be a new
surprise for me to find.

When I got home from camp, I tried to hide my body from my parents.

**One day we all
went swimming at
my uncle's house**

and I shaved my armpits with an electric razor.

I cut them up pretty bad.

In the end I said that I didn't feel like going swimming.

It's hard for me
to understand this
behavior now.

I suppose it had a lot to do with wanting to stay a child.

Never wanting any change.

Fixed in time

like a character from a movie.

I have never felt excitement about getting older.

Until now.

I am filled with optimism about the future.

This sense
that my life
is unfolding
before me

on the start of a journey.

Looking in the mirror

I am finally at peace with the idea that this grown-up face

is me.

My grandfather and I used to play a game called Drunk Driving.

We would sail his enormous luxury sedan down an abandoned Palm Springs boulevard

swerving quickly from side to side

while my tiny body would tumble across the back seat

to our endless laughter.

to stir endless laughter

My Grandpa Phil

is the only
grandparent
I have ever
really known.

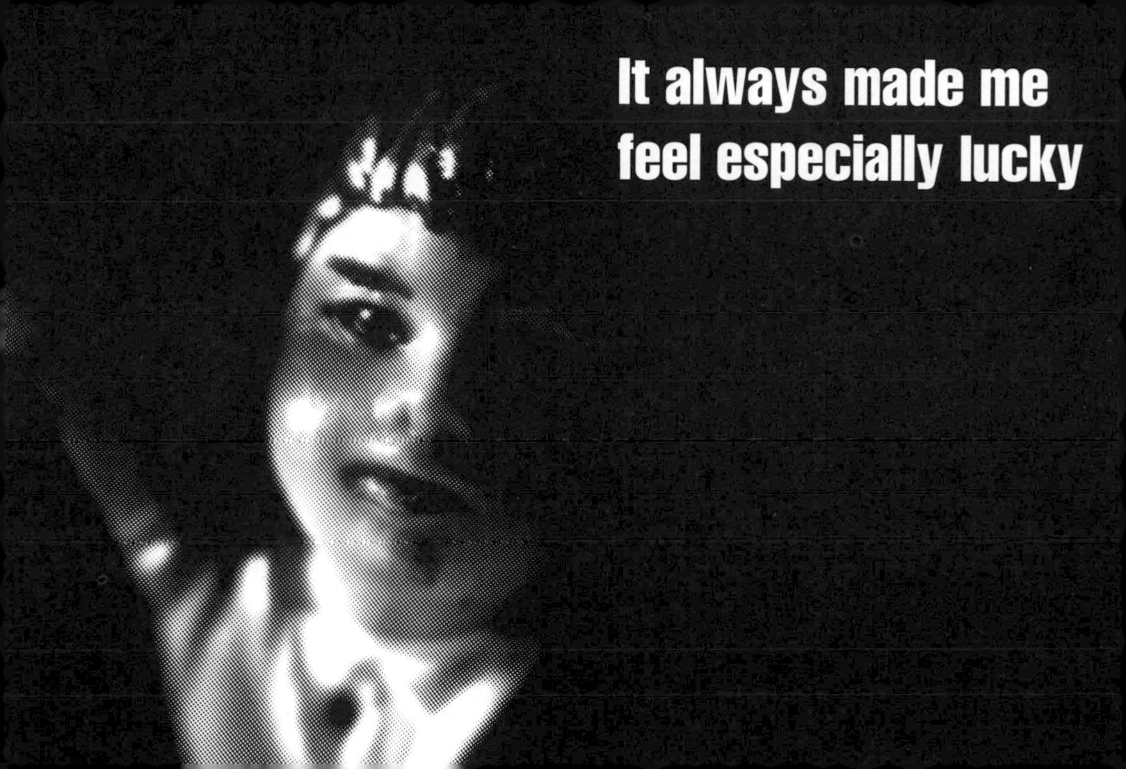
It always made me
feel especially lucky

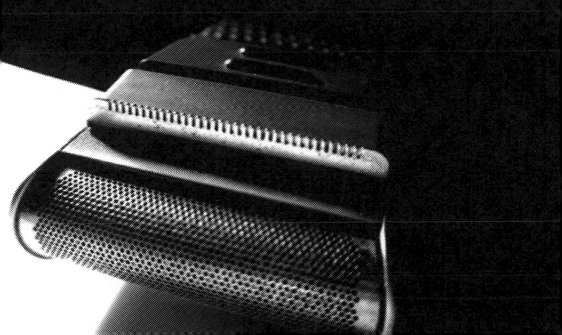

to have my very own grown-up

who would shoot me a wink

as he swiped me
pieces of caramel
in the grocery store

while my mother pretended not to notice.

My grandfather taught me magic.

My grandfather caught the magic.

To this day I still carry around some magic in my pocket

FIG II

in the hope that
I can pull it out
and amaze you.

I have my grandfather's forehead.

Which means that sooner or later, I'll probably have to call the Hair Club for Men.

This is the kind
of joke that would
make him chuckle.

So these two fagalas
are sitting in a bar.

And in comes this ripe tomato. And she is absolutely amazing.

Really svelte.

And one looks at the other and says,

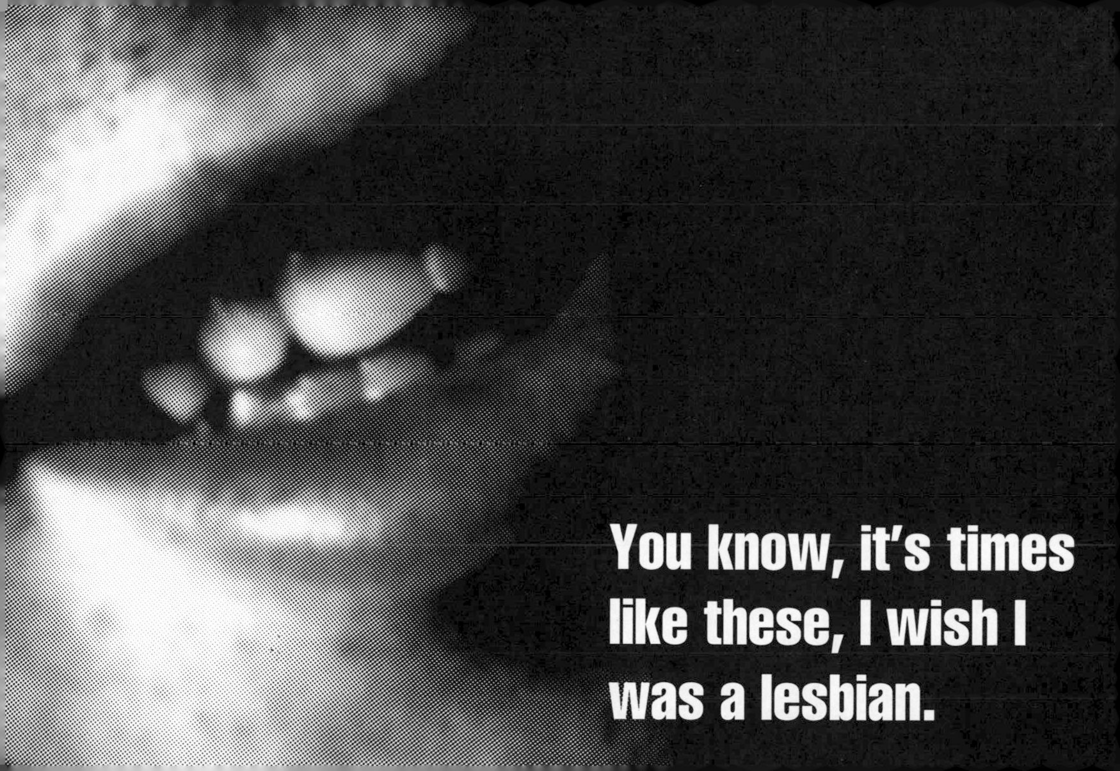
You know, it's times like these, I wish I was a lesbian.

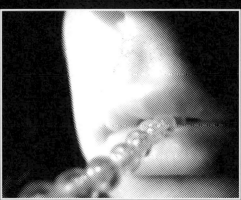

We do a lot of laughing at my house.

It's much easier than crying.

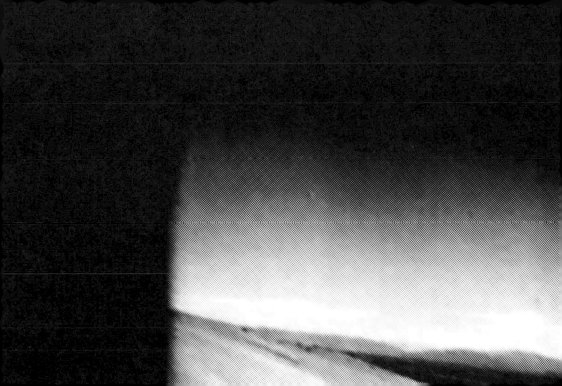

When I was 11,
I went down to Palm
Springs to visit my
grandfather alone.

He picked me up at the airport and before we even went home,

he stopped
to buy me
a present.

"Joshey," he used to say. "I'm gonna buy you the whole world."

I knew he meant it.

We pulled into an enormous shopping mall.

We pulled into
the cities
leaving mail.

He led me over to the boy's toy aisle.

He let me take my time.

We walked back to the car.

And from nowhere it began.

Mom says that you're seeing a

PSYCHIATRIST.

(sic-chi-a-trist)

SHE says you're **AFRAID.**

What do **YOU** have to be afraid of?

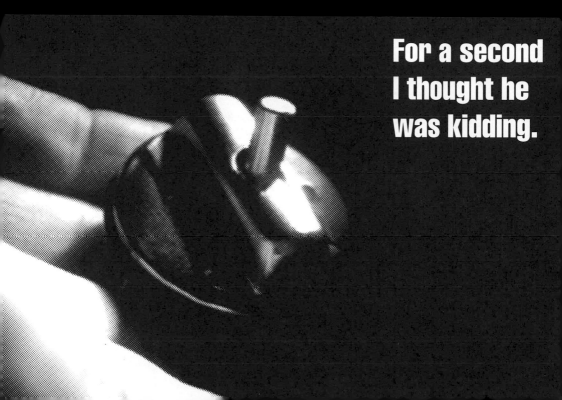

For a second
I thought he
was kidding.

What do you talk to her about?
What do you tell her?
TELL ME!
What do you tell her
that you can't tell me?
Do you hear?   ANSWER ME.

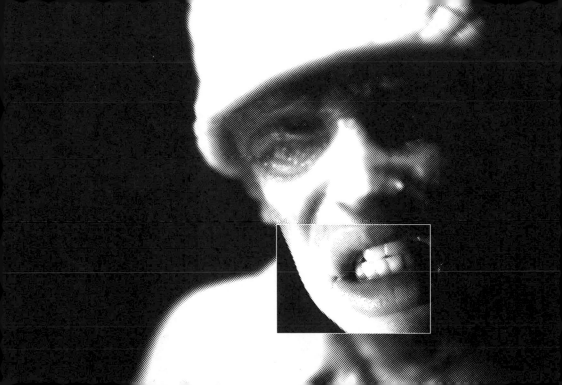

Mom tells me
you're afraid.
Are you?

sometimes.

You can't go
crying to some
head shrinker
your whole life.

You better get strong, because the world is—

Look at me.

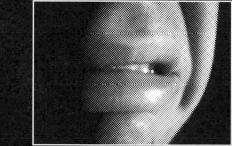

We sat in the parking lot for more than an hour.

We sat in the parking lot for more than an hour.

I WANT YOU TO GO HOME AND TELL YOUR PSYCHIATRIST TO GO FLY A KITE. **DO YOU HEAR ME?** CALL YOUR MOM AND TELL HER THAT YOU DON'T WANT TO GO ANYMORE.

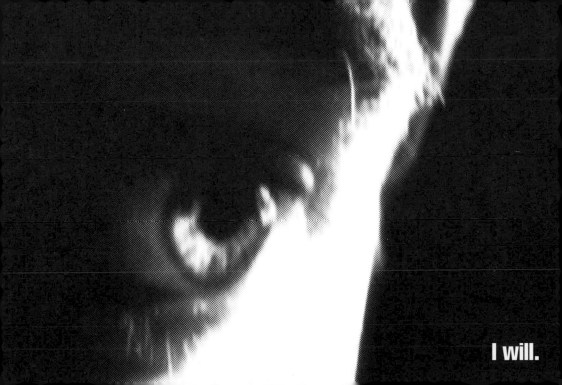

I will.

He dropped the bag in my lap.

And we drove away.

I spent most of that vacation watching TV.

For a long time,
I was angry.

I was alone?

Our contact was minimal.

Years later, as I stood
waiting at the gate
for his plane to arrive

I decided that I was going to confront him.

When I saw him,
he was so excited
to see me that
when he leaned
over to kiss me,

his lips made this weird smacking sound.

I laughed.

I make the exact same sound when I kiss.

And just then

I felt the anger pass from my body.

I didn't want it anymore.

Rage has
this way of
disappearing

when you think you need it most.

When you think you need it most.

My grandfather tells an old story.

A Catholic Priest, a Protestant Minister and a Rabbi were asked the question, "When does Life begin?"

The Priest answers first. "Life," he says, "begins at conception."

Then the Minister answers, "We believe that life begins once the child leaves the womb."

The Rabbi thinks for a long time. "When does life begin?" he says.

"When the dog dies and the kids move out."

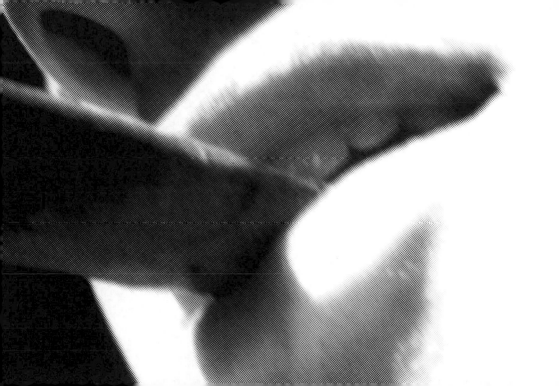

When I was 13,

I stopped being affectionate towards my mother.

I never said anything

but my kisses

became more and more infrequent.

I was suddenly insecure around her body.

Uncomfortable with her touch.

I know this had a
lot to do with my
sexual awakening.

I was choosing sides.

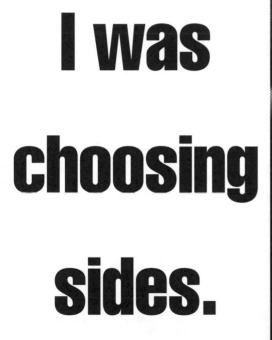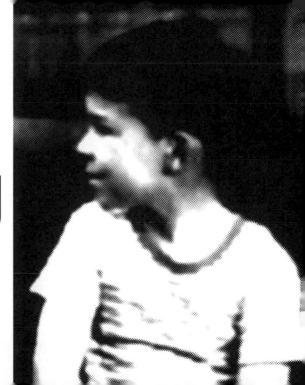

In a move towards what I knew to be normal,

I decided that my mother could not be a sexual object.

As mothers

often are.

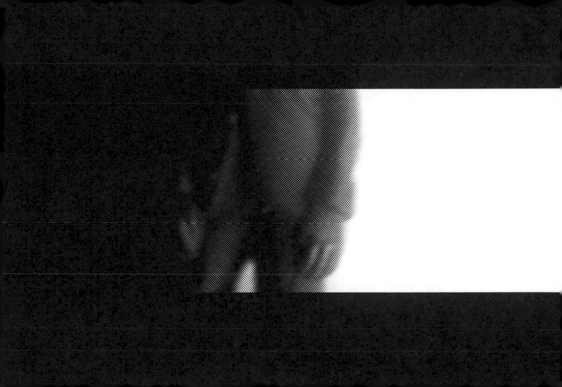

Time has its way
with insecurity

and somehow we forget

our sleepless nights.

I was at a wedding a few months ago.

It was a slow song.

The kind where all
of the sons dance
with the mothers.

And we were dancing.

I had my hand
pressed firmly
against her waist.

For a moment I thought
about the way I was
touching her.

I hadn't touched
my mother like
this since I was
a child.

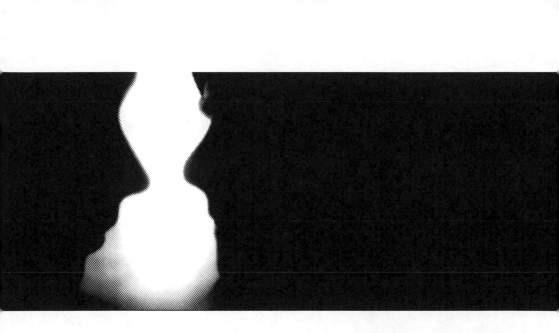

But it was okay.

And I was looking into her eyes,

and it was
suddenly very
clear to me.

I was created by this woman.

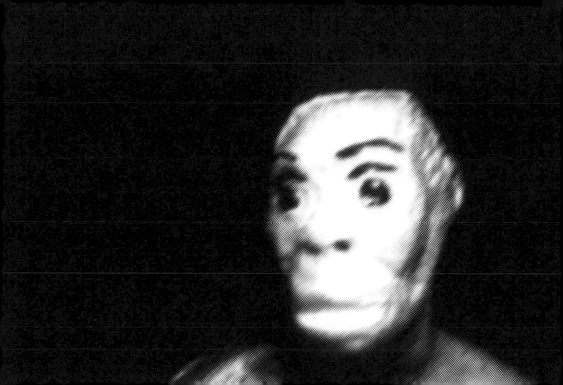

She brought me life.

I lived inside of her.

We had been one body.

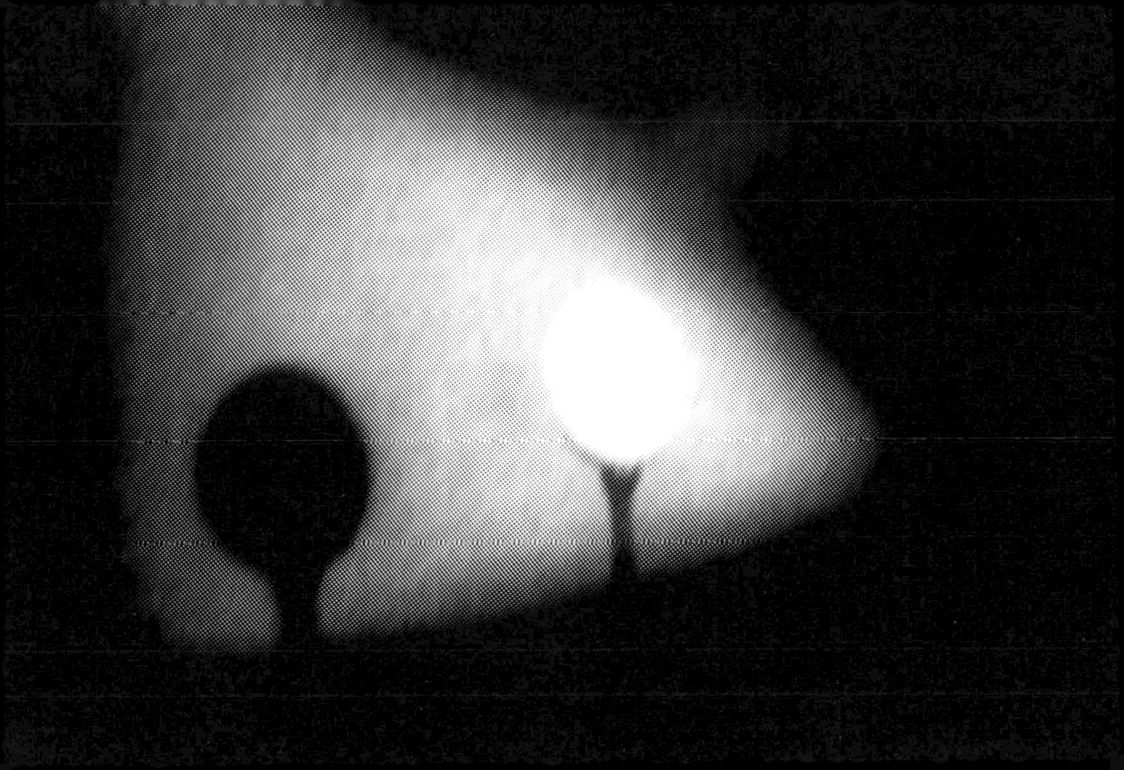

In my own
piecemeal
version of
spirituality,

it is a most sacred notion
to know your maker.

And to dance with her.

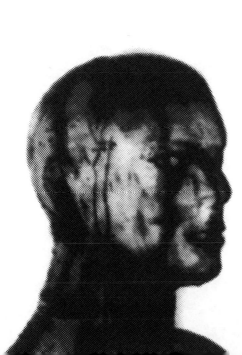

She asked me what I was thinking about and I told her.

"Yeah. Well, you can't go back."

These words run through my head a lot these days,

as I approach the symbolic end of my childhood.

I have this fear that in growing up,

I am losing my home

and I will never
again know the
warmth that
I knew as a child.

That I still long for.

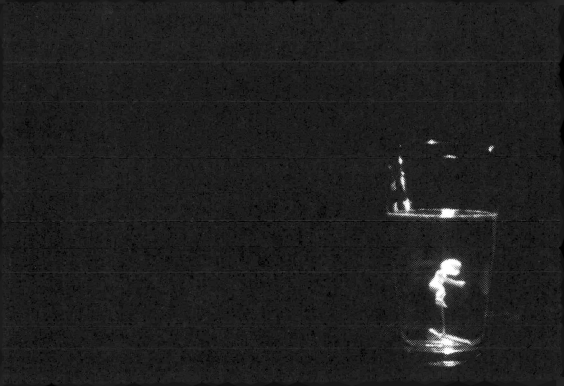

The End

A MONOGRAM
PRODUCTION

I would like to express my gratitude to two photo archives for their generous support, without which this book would not have been possible.

My humble
thanks to:

Rick Prelinger and his Ephemeral Films. I have been your fan since I was 13 and I had to beg my mother for the hundred dollars to buy Quicktime 1.0. It was through your imagery that I first found the tools to tell these stories. I thank you for your keen sense of humor and eye for detail.

and

Dave Shemarin of Wrightwood Laboratories, who has valiantly preserved choice morsels of Americana in his hilarious CD collections of TV commercials from the 40s through the 70s. Check him out at www.wrightwood.com.

Many more thanks

To the people who made this book: First to Doug Gayeton, who brought me to my friends at Melcher Media. To Dick Waller, who introduced me to Susan Grode, who has disproven every lawyer joke I ever heard. To Duncan Bock and Charlie Melcher, who first sold this unconventional book and then stuck by it and me; and to Gillian Sowell, Andrea Hirsh, Molly Cooper and Megan Worman. To my heroes at HarperCollins, Joseph Montebello, Cathy Hemming and Laurie Rippon. To my Teachers: Wendy Snauffer, who guided me through the first incarnation of these stories; Dr. Marjorie Barnett, who served as the catalyst for these stories to be told; and Harriet Cholden, Dr. Marie Stone, Bill Duffy, Pat McHale, Bernard Markwell, Charlie Kanwischer and Stanley Rabinowitz, who all added years to my educational life. To all my friends: Emily Shelton, Jason Gill, Michael Barrett, Emil Wolmut, Rob Bernstein, Liz Hammond, Ron "Fat Sammy" Deutsch, Cameron Holtzman, Robert Tercek, Tom Gibbons, Jin Kang, Nina Goodman, Valerie Roche, Amy Baily, Ethan Adelman and all my friends at Oxygen Media who make coming to work a pleasure. And to my family: My dear sweet C; T and B, who have always brought cornflakes to family events; my favorite Grandfather in the world; and of course my mother, father, Theo and Jonah: I wrote this book because I could no longer keep my love on the inside.

This book was produced by Melcher Media, Inc., New York City.

Charles Melcher, Publisher
Duncan Bock, Editor
Gillian Sowell, Editorial Manager
Andrea Hirsh, Director of Production
Molly Cooper, Editorial Assistant

Special thanks to Megan Worman for her invaluable support.

Published by Perennial in association with Melcher Media. Perennial is an imprint of HarperCollins*Publishers*.

Good / Grief. Copyright © 2000 by Josh Koppel. All rights reserved. Printed in China. No part of this book may be used or reproduced in any manner whatsoever without written permission except in the case of brief quotations embodied in critical articles and reviews. For information address HarperCollins Publishers, Inc., 10 East 53rd Street, New York, NY 10022.

HarperCollins books may be purchased for educational, business, or sales promotional use. For information please write: Special Markets Department, HarperCollins Publishers, Inc., 10 East 53rd Street, New York, NY 10022.

FIRST EDITION

10 9 8 7 6 5 4 3 2 1

ISBN 0-06-095628-3

Library of Congress Cataloging-in-Publication Data is available.